Optimal Tennis

Jack L. Groppel
& Arthur Shay

D1566083

Contemporary Books, Inc.
Chicago

Library of Congress Cataloging in Publication Data

Groppel, Jack L.
    Optimal tennis.

    Includes index.
    1. Tennis.   I. Shay, Arthur.   II. Title.
GV995.G75   1983   796.342   83-1935
ISBN 0-8092-5602-9

Published by Contemporary Books, Inc.
180 North Michigan Avenue, Chicago, Illinois 60601
Manufactured in the United States of America
Library of Congress Catalog Card Number: 83-1935
International Standard Book Number: 0-8092-5602-9

Published simultaneously in Canada by
Beaverbooks, Ltd.
150 Lesmill Road
Don Mills, Ontario M3B 2T5
Canada

For Asher and Irene Birnbaum, who founded *Tennis Magazine,* who have quietly contributed their intelligence and skills to their favorite sport, and whose joyous labors are reflected in its growth.

Arthur Shay

Contents

Preface

Time and time again, I go to the public tennis courts and watch all the players attempting to imitate their idols on the pro tour. I'll never forget, following John McEnroe's debut on television, how many juniors the next day were trying to imitate his serving stance. I seriously don't think one ball went over the net in the five or ten minutes that I was watching. With so many players searching for winning techniques to imitate and improve their games, the question, "What is perfect tennis?" should be addressed.

As a person interested in the efficiency of human motion, and with an extensive background in the playing and coaching of tennis, I am always intrigued when I hear players and teaching pros discuss the *best* way to play tennis. I'm not sure there really is a best way, but some ways of playing are better than others. With that in mind, we went about writing this text for you, the tennis player who's looking for the perfect form.

Most tennis books dealing with the instructional aspects of tennis are concerned with perfection, but show the perfect way to play by using models who merely stand in static positions while having their pictures taken. That is one way to show how the game should be played, but it leaves out many facets of tennis that must be utilized when you are unable to get completely set to hit the ball. For that reason, we combined the effectiveness of using models to demonstrate certain aspects of tennis with the performance techniques of professional tennis players during competition. By using the competitive techniques of these athletes, we feel that you will receive the most complete instruction possible from a book.

This book covers all of the basic strokes you will encounter when playing a competitive tennis match—information that can be beneficial for all levels of players from beginner to tournament competitor.

Acknowledgments

Several people deserve credit for their substantial influence on my career and this book:

Those who have helped me learn about the game of tennis—Bill Wicks, Chet Milford, Vic Braden, and the tennis community of Alton, Illinois.

The professors who greatly influenced my academic career—Chuck Dillman, Bob Singer, and Terry Ward.

The pros who taught me how to work with skilled athletes—Tim Gullikson, Tom Gullikson, and Stan Smith.

The people and organizations who contributed their time and effort to the pictures in this book—Rick and Jo Ann Vetter, Fred Marchese, The Chicago Aces, The Right Club of Schaumburg, Illinois, and the numerous tennis pros whose athletic ability made this book possible.

The individuals who assisted me by typing and collating this manuscript—Barb Young and Terri Bodecker.

And, finally, those who continue to encourage me and provide support—my parents, my sister and her family, along with my very close friend, Sue Arildsen.

Jack L. Groppel, Ph.D.

1
Playing Your Best Tennis

Striving for perfection! Just about anybody who plays the game of tennis has, at one time or another, wanted to work on specific aspects of the game to improve his or her play as much as possible. Some of us go to incredible lengths trying to perfect our tennis games, especially when we dream about all the money won on the professional tour and how we might share in it if only our backhands were a little better. Many people, however, don't have the opportunity to improve that is available to others. The fortunate ones have coaches who assist them in correcting their strokes and in monitoring their match play, but others who don't have a good skills coach have to struggle along with trial and error, swinging the racket in every motion possible until they find the style that seems to work best for them.

Think about when you play your best tennis.

Is it following the finals of a major televised tennis match? Is it right after you've had a lesson from the club pro? Or maybe it's early in the morning, following one of your dreams about winning Wimbledon! There really is something psychological that happens to all of us when we go through any of these situations. It always seems that we can play our best tennis after we've experienced some type of euphoric feeling about the game. However, once the euphoria is gone, the problem then becomes how *should* we best hit the ball? For example, if we see Borg win on television, should we all at once begin using looping topspin shots and try to roll the racket over the ball as many commentators say he does? Or if Connors wins, should we then try to pulverize every shot by jumping into the ball as we swing? If that's the case, our game style would change from week to week. And since that meth-

Notice how the body parts work together in Butch Walts' service motion.

1   2

od of style selection wouldn't be the best to use, there must be another way of figuring out how to play our best tennis.

Although the pros play with specific idiosyncrasies and different styles—hitting the ball with high, looping topspins or driving the ball with low screamers barely clearing the net—there are numerous things we can learn from watching how these elite performers play the game. For example, by observing how they generate force to effectively swing the racket, you can improve your game significantly. With that in mind, let's examine how the human body works while playing the game of tennis.

GROUND REACTION FORCE

When a player swings to hit a tennis ball, a complex series of events has to occur. First of all, much of the force in swinging a tennis racket comes from the ground. I know this may be hard to believe, since the part of the body most often associated with hitting the ball is the arm. However, it's a fact that you must have a significant *ground reaction force* to swing effectively into impact. Why else would skilled tennis players

flex and extend their knees prior to serving? You can see in the photographs above and on page 3 how this ground reaction force is generated and then transferred from the ground through the body to the racket. As Butch Walts tosses the ball, you can see how the legs are bent at the knee. As the forward swing is initiated, notice the extension of the legs and how the hips begin to turn toward the net. These are the first two steps in hitting an effective serve. The ground reaction force is generated by the flexion and extension of the knees, which in turn transfers that force into the hips, which begin rotating. From this point, the force generated by the rotating hips is transferred to the trunk, which then begins rotating. The trunk action is obvious if you notice how the trunk position turns slightly backward as Walts begins his service motion, and then compare that to the trunk position when the ball is struck. Therefore, the third step in generating effective force to hit a serve is rotation of the trunk. From this point, the force is transferred from the trunk to the arm, which creates a great amount of velocity in bringing the racket across toward impact. Thus, when players become skilled in the game of tennis, they can usually employ all of their body parts in an optimal fashion. They have learned, through a great deal of practice, to

3   4   5

properly sequence the action of the various body parts involved in transferring the force from the ground all the way out to the racket.

Although professional tennis players are the most proficient tennis players in the world at performing various tennis skills, there are still numerous idiosyncrasies that exist among them which should not be imitated by beginning players. For example, many players can get away with performing various skills without utilizing their bodies to the greatest advantage. One of the biggest topics of discussion at the 1982 Wimbledon tennis final between John McEnroe and Jimmy Connors was the fact that Jimmy Connors had changed his serve. However, few could understand what he had done differently nor why he was serving so much harder than before. When questioned about the change in his serve, Jimmy replied that he was trying to toss the ball farther in front of his body to get more extension and reach into the court. If you looked at old films of Jimmy's former serve, you would see that he used to toss the ball directly overhead, and as he would initiate his forward swing and generate the ground reaction force, his rear leg would stay in place behind his body and would not allow a proper amount of hip rotation. This enabled Jimmy to have a fantastic spin serve but

caused a lot of problems when he tried to hit a fast cannonball serve. By tossing the ball farther into the court, he forced his body to rotate around toward the court more. This enabled him to generate more hip rotation, which in turn was transferred into the trunk and finally to the arm. Therefore, the key to Connor's effective serving in the 1982 Wimbledon final was not only the fact that he was tossing the ball farther into the court to facilitate his body extension, but also the fact that by doing so, he was able to increase his hip and trunk rotation and generate more force as he hit the ball.

To understand how the human body most efficiently swings a tennis racket, you must realize that the ground reaction force generated at the feet is incredibly important. Without the proper amount of force from the ground, you'll never be able to play the game effectively. Remember, however, that the goal of a good tennis player is to hit forcefully yet with control. You don't want to hit with maximum force like a home run hitter, but with enough force and control intermixed to keep the opponent always on the defensive. With this information in mind, the following chapters will discuss how top tennis players prepare to move for the ball and hit such effective strokes.

2

The Keys for Proper Footwork

Try to visualize what you feel is proper footwork as you move to hit a ball. Right away, most of us envision the ball bouncing nice and easy at about waist height. Then we see ourselves pivot and step across to hit the "perfect" ground stroke. But seriously, how many times do you think a ball will bounce with little velocity at waist height?

Tennis is a game of emergencies! No two shots in a match may be the same. Consider the fact that a ball could be hit as a low, hard drive; a looping moon ball; a high lob; a drop shot; or an angled half-volley. It could be hit with a great deal of topspin, underspin, or sidespin. The list continues, but these examples illustrate various situations that occur in the game of tennis that you may have to adapt your body to in order to play well. Therefore, knowing the number of different situations that can arise when you play a set of tennis (whether it is in the finals of a

tournament or against the guy next door) will help you fully understand how to best move your body comfortably and efficiently to quickly cover a tennis court. The next question is, once you get to the ball, how do you move your feet to hit it most effectively? Let's begin from that point.

THE READY POSITION

Prior to hitting a ball, most players have a "set" position they assume. This "ready position" should enable them to move with equal quickness in any direction on the court. The key purpose of the ready position is that it allows players to get their center of gravity slightly lower than normal, increasing their base of support. At the top of page 6, you can see how Mary Lou Piatek prepares for a return of serve and for a volley. In both cases, the knees are slightly flexed; the ma-

Mary Lou Piatek achieving a ready position for a return of serve and when at the net.

jority of the body weight is placed over the balls of the feet. Notice how the racket is positioned in front of the body.

The importance of a ready position has been seriously questioned by many people who feel that as long as the player is "aware" of the opponent's return, there is no need to achieve a definite ready position. This may be true for the highly skilled professional, but I doubt whether a beginning tennis player should try only to be aware of an oncoming ball. Therefore, let's examine what a ready position should look like.

In the photographs below of Piatek assuming a ready position at the net and a ready position when returning a serve, notice that her knees are slightly flexed and the majority of her body weight is on the balls of her feet. The occurrence that follows probably raises more questions than anything else in the game of tennis. Why does a player take a slight hop into the air in getting set for the return as Mary Lou demonstrates in this sequence?

Mary Lou Piatek demonstrates the footwork involved in preparing for a return.

UNWEIGHTING

When tennis players move from a ready position to prepare for a tennis stroke, a certain amount of "unweighting" must occur. This unweighting is commonly seen in many other sport activities, like surfing and skiing. As tennis players get set in the ready position (as Sandy Collins demonstrates below), the majority of their body weight should be over the balls of the feet. Once they recognize which side of their body the opponent's shot has been hit toward, they quickly drop their center of gravity by rapidly flexing the knees. This sudden drop decreases the force of the feet against the ground and allows the body to shift its position. Once the unweighting has occurred, many athletes will either move in preparation for the shot or take another slight hop to further prepare themselves. The purpose of the hop is to be perfectly timed and set the leg mus-

Sandy Collins showing the footwork necessary in hitting the return of serve.

1   2   3

4   5   6

1

2

3

Mary Lou Piatek demonstrates how the unit turn helps her body rotation when returning serve. Observe how her left foot has fired out to the side in the second picture.

cles in preparation for movement. Therefore, many tennis players unweight, take a slight hop, set the muscles, and prepare to hit the stroke.

If you've seen Tracy Austin, you may have noticed that she moves around like a little jack-rabbit between shots. That much body action may not be necessary, but if you wish to play good tennis, you must have good footwork to run for a shot. If you don't have to run for the ball, you still must synchronize your feet with the stroke to be hit. That phase in movement is commonly known as the *unit turn*.

THE UNIT TURN

The term *unit turn* was coined by two tennis

4

5

6

7

coaches at Harvard University, David Fish and Don Usher. They observed that when skilled tennis players move to prepare for a stroke, the first action is *not* to "take the racket back." The first movement observed for skilled competitors occurs at the feet. Sandy Collins (page 7) and Mary Lou Piatek (page 8) demonstrate this extremely well. The foot on the side of the body toward which the ball is traveling is lifted completely off the ground and rotated toward the sideline. This unit turn causes that entire side of the body to rotate in that direction, which causes a slight forward imbalance and *also* takes the racket back. Therefore, don't think of stroke preparation as merely taking the racket back; think of it as the unit turn. Then you will not only have the racket back in preparation for the swing but your entire body will be adequately prepared for movement into the stroke.

THE STROKE

The Step Across

Once the unit turn has been accomplished, you must create enough force to effectively hit the stroke. There are two methods of footwork for correctly hitting a tennis stroke once you are properly prepared. The first is the most commonly known technique: the classic crossover step as you swing, which transfers your body weight directly toward the point of impact. As shown in the photographs on page 10, you can see how this player has oriented his body to step across into the shot. He has already employed the unit turn and appears as though he is about to fall forward. This slight forward imbalance is a direct benefit of the unit turn because it allows the player to swing the racket effectively if he's rushed by a bad bounce or some other uncontrolled factor. From this position of forward imbalance, he merely steps across and swings the racket toward the ball. The step across, however, is crucial as far as timing is concerned. When you are ready to hit an approaching ball, you must remember a certain rhythm: step, then swing. If there is too much time between the step forward and the swinging action, you will not get an effective transfer of momentum to the stroke. If the step occurs at the same time as the swing

forward, there will not be ample time to transfer that momentum, either. Therefore, the movement must be rhythmical (step, then swing) with a definite but not lingering separation between the two.

The Open Stance

The other method of footwork that can be utilized in getting set for a stroke is the "open stance." The open stance stroke is used by many players on the professional tour. Borg, for example, seldom uses the step across method of hitting a forehand. He almost always uses an open stance forehand and no one is going to say that Borg's forehand is weak! To hit an open stance forehand, you simply step to the side (in contrast to stepping across) in striking the ball. There really is little transfer of linear momentum in the open stance ground stroke (as you see when using a closed stance) but the use of body rotation can be phenomenal. Few of us ever see the way a pro tennis player sets up to hit an open stance ground stroke. We only see the final product when the professional player is facing the net during the stroke or in the follow-through. Notice the player on page 11 as he sets up to hit an open stance forehand. The leg on the side toward which the ball is traveling steps farther to the side and the hip and trunk are actually facing that same side. Now watch as the player swings forward to make contact with the ball. As impact is approached, the hips and then the trunk rotate to bring the arm and racket in position for impact. As you can see, a player does not hit an open-stance ground stroke by merely facing the net and swinging the racket. There is an incredible amount of body rotation used to bring the racket effectively toward ball contact.

The major problem with this type of stroke, however, is the lack of control that most of us have when we try to hit with this technique. In the step across method, we are always taught to hit over the front foot or slightly ahead of the front foot. With the open-stance ground stroke, there is no front foot that most of us need for a crutch. Therefore, where should ball contact occur? It needs to occur ahead of the body but the location at which it should occur depends on the timing and the type of stroke desired. For exam-

Rick Vetter, tournament player and teaching professional, illustrating a closed stance ground stroke.

Rick Vetter shows how to hit a ground stroke with an open stance. Notice the hip and trunk rotation involved.

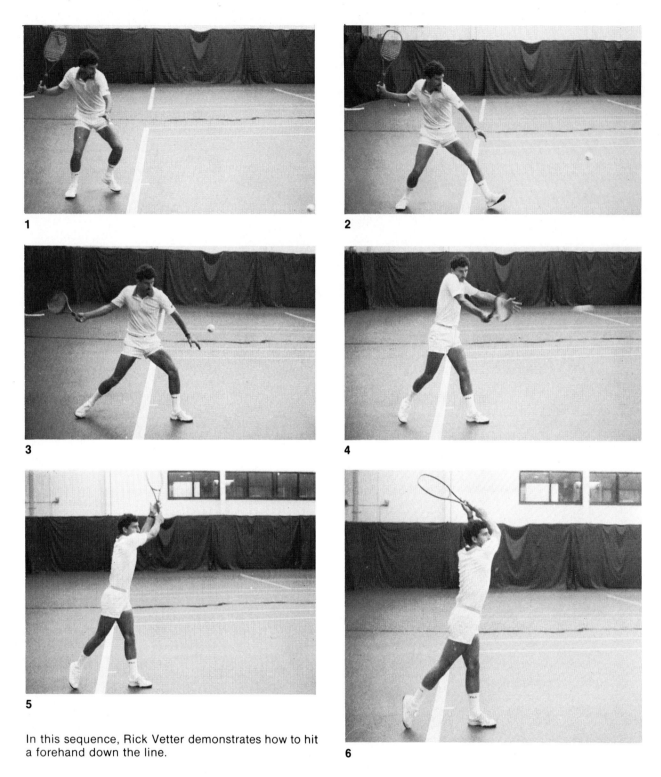

In this sequence, Rick Vetter demonstrates how to hit a forehand down the line.

ple, if you are hitting down the line as the player above is, the ball will probably be contacted nearly even with the body. And notice in the follow-through how the shoulders are turned fairly open *in the direction of the stroke*. If the ball is to be hit crosscourt (next page), it will be hit earlier and more in front of the body. Again, take note of the shoulder turn. The shoulder turn is extremely important because it controls the force and direction of the shot, but it isn't as easy

1

2

3

4

6

5

7

Notice the body rotation and the timing involved when hitting a ground stroke crosscourt.

1

2

3

4

Photos 1–8: Observe the quick initial side-step action involved when moving laterally to prepare for the return. Once you near the point of impact, you can easily step into the shot.

as it looks. That's why most players who attempt an open-stance ground stroke spray the ball in all directions.

One of these two types of footwork—closed stance or open stance—is necessary when preparing for a stroke. However, getting to the point where preparation can begin is often a problem for many people. They simply don't know how to run for a shot.

The Lateral Step

You will never be in a tennis match where you don't have to run to return a shot, even if the ball is only a few feet to your side. However, you may not necessarily need to use an all-out sprint. When tennis players stand at the middle of the baseline awaiting their opponents' returns, they usually employ some type of ready position. If they recognize that the ball may land as far as ten feet to the side, they can utilize various forms of footwork to quickly cover the court. One extremely efficient method that can be used is a lateral side step maneuver. In the photos above and on the next page, notice how this competitor moves laterally to hit his return. There are a couple of quick side steps, then the unit turn is employed in a pivoting action. From this position, the player can either hit with an open stance or move to step across and into the shot as you see in the photographic sequence.

Sprinting for a Return and The Recovery Step

Often, the ball will not be hit directly to your side so a lateral movement pattern won't do you

5

6

7

8

any good. In cases such as this, you will have to sprint to hit the ball. Let's say you have to hit a stroke from a running position and go for a winner down the line. Notice how the athlete on pages 16–17 sprints to hit exactly that shot. Observe the timing involved between the footwork and the swing to hit the most effective stroke. As he pushes off with the rear foot, the body is off-balance forward. The racket is taken back and the swing forward occurs following the push off with the rear foot. Now, watch what happens once the ball has been hit. Most of us never see this part because we watch the ball travel back across the net and the movements of the opponent in preparing to return the shot. However, we can learn quite a bit by observing how a skilled athlete recovers from a sprinting maneuver to return to an advantageous court position. Once this athlete has hit the ball, he quickly "puts the brakes on," and his rear foot (the one he pushed off with to generate force to swing the racket) is brought around to the side so it provides the major braking mechanism. Observe what happens once that foot is planted into the ground. There is a slight push off back toward the middle of the court so the athlete can recover most efficiently. Fortunately, he hit a winner down the line so his recovery wasn't that essential. On page 17, you can see Mary Lou Piatek exhibiting this recovery step very well.

The one problem that many people have in attempting this type of footwork is that they bring the rear foot around too quickly. The purpose of allowing the rear foot to rotate around the body is not only to provide the most effective braking mechanism but also to allow sufficient

1

2

3

4

5

6

7

8

Photos 1–11: Sometimes you have to actually sprint to hit a return. Notice the timing from when the athlete ceases the running stride to initiate the footwork in hitting an effective ground stroke down the line. Although you may be forced to hit a ball on a dead run, always try to maintain control over your upper body.

9

10

11

body rotation into the stroke. If that rear leg is brought around too soon, the body "opens up" much too quickly and the results of the shot could be poor.

You must understand the timing involved in

order to use this movement effectively in improving your own footwork and tennis game in general. It is a timed maneuver that skilled athletes can employ with ease, but that timing must be learned through practice, practice, practice.

Mary Lou Piatek illustrates the recovery step movement for both her forehand and two-handed backhand. Notice how the rear foot is brought around *after* ball contact.

3

The Forehand Drive

Many people feel that the forehand drive is the easiest stroke in the game of tennis. Perhaps it's because the forehand is the first stroke taught by most professionals. It is also a stroke that allows your body to be "open" into the shot, whereas other strokes do not permit this sort of body movement.

FOREHAND GRIPS

Before discussing exactly how a correct forehand drive should be hit, we need to examine the various ways of holding the racket to hit an effective ground stroke.

The Western Forehand Grip

One grip, commonly seen on the professional tour, is the western forehand grip. As shown at the right, make a V between the thumb and fore-

The western forehand grip.

When holding the racket with a western forehand grip so your hand is oriented as though you were shaking hands, you can see how the racket face is slightly "closed."

The Continental Grip

A second grip that can be used for the forehand drive is the continental grip. If you make a V between the thumb and forefinger of your swinging hand and position the V on the left beveled edge of the racket handle (for a right-handed player), most of your hand will be placed on top of the racket handle. This grip has evolved from the British and Australian players who have basically learned to play tennis on grass and other extremely fast surfaces which are conducive to very low bounces. It is used on a

The continental grip.

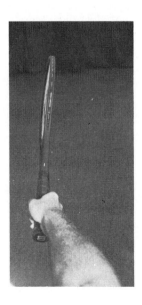

Notice how the racket face is slightly "open" as the racket is held with a continental grip.

finger of your swinging hand. Now, place your hand so that the V is on the right beveled edge of the racket handle (for a right-handed player). This positions the hand so that the palm is behind the racket as the racket is swung forward. The main advantage to using a western forehand grip is the fact that a great amount of topspin— an aggressive-type maneuver—can be hit with ease. Another advantage is that high-bouncing balls can also be hit without too much trouble. One severe problem of the western forehand grip, however, is that low-bouncing balls can be difficult to return due to how the racket is oriented in the hand. If you hold the racket directly in front of your body, the racket face is slightly "closed." When a ball bounces very low, contact must occur much ahead of the body to hit it effectively. If contact doesn't occur well in front, the ball will be projected downward and into the net.

fast surface because the racket face is naturally "open" at ball contact. You can see this slightly open racket face illustrated at the bottom of page 20, as this person holds the racket directly in front of his body. Opening the racket face easily allows the ball to be hit upward over the net following its usual low bounce. However, the main disadvantage of the continental grip is that few tournaments are currently played on grass, so there is little need for an open racket face at ball contact. Because the ball usually bounces much higher on clay than on grass, the racket face must be nearly vertical to the ground at each impact. To get the racket to a near-vertical position using a continental grip, a certain amount of racket head rotation must occur during the forward swing. This creates the natural problem of timing the racket swing so it will contact the ball at the correct position relative to your body. This problem is further compounded once the player begins to feel more strain during a match. Imagine the pressure in timing the racket head rotation to a near-vertical impact position when you are in the finals of a tournament and the score is 5–5 in the third set. In fact, if you happen to be watching a match between highly skilled tennis players using continental grips, and the score gets very close, you will often see them use less ball velocity and more topspin to make sure the ball is kept in the court. This compensation affects their match play and can be detrimental to their final performance.

The Eastern Forehand Grip

The final grip is the eastern forehand grip. Many teaching pros feel that this grip is the most mechanically efficient out of the three possible types of forehand grips. Make the V between your thumb and forefinger of your swinging hand. Then place your swinging hand on the handle so that the V is directly on top of the flat portion of the grip as you hold the racket face vertical. The reason why many authorities feel this grip is so effective is that it places the hand in such a position on the racket handle that no racket head rotation need occur to hit a ball. For example, hold the racket directly in front of you with an eastern forehand grip as though you were shaking hands with a friend. The racket

The eastern forehand grip.

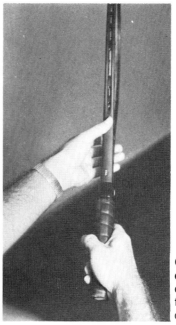

Observe how the eastern forehand grip causes the racket face to be near vertical.

face should be straight up and down relative to the ground. This vertical racket face is extremely important to the game of tennis and illustrates why the eastern forehand grip may be the most suitable for you to use.

THE FOREHAND STROKE

The Closed Stance

Once you've decided on the grip type to use, you need to learn how the racket must be swung

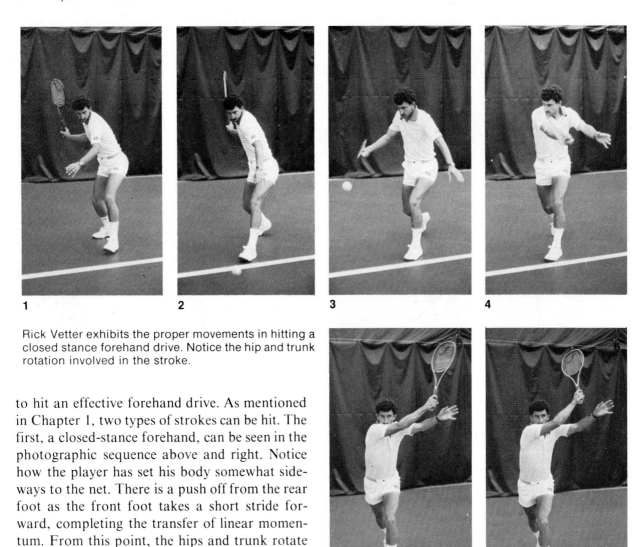

1   2   3   4

Rick Vetter exhibits the proper movements in hitting a closed stance forehand drive. Notice the hip and trunk rotation involved in the stroke.

5   6

to hit an effective forehand drive. As mentioned in Chapter 1, two types of strokes can be hit. The first, a closed-stance forehand, can be seen in the photographic sequence above and right. Notice how the player has set his body somewhat sideways to the net. There is a push off from the rear foot as the front foot takes a short stride forward, completing the transfer of linear momentum. From this point, the hips and trunk rotate to bring the racket head into impact and the player finishes with a nice, high follow-through.

The Open Stance

The second type of forehand drive you can hit is called the open-stance forehand. On page 23, you can see the same player preparing to hit this stroke. Notice the difference in preparation from the closed stance. The upper body is somewhat sideways to the net but the legs are actually separated parallel to the net. This is where many people get confused about the use of an open-stance ground stroke. Since the upper body is sideways to the net, it allows a great deal of hip and trunk rotation into the stroke. You can see in the sequence how this player begins with the upper body toward the sideline and generates hip and trunk rotation through the legs to swing the racket head toward ball contact. Notice that the

follow-through is very similar to that used for a closed-stance forehand—high in order to assist in propelling the ball over the net.

SPIN

Once the correct techniques are mastered, you should learn some of the various strategies of hitting a ball to keep the opponent off guard. One way of doing that is to hit with spin, whether it's topspin or underspin.

Right: As an open stance forehand is demonstrated, notice the rotation that occurs at the hips and trunk in preparation for the stroke.

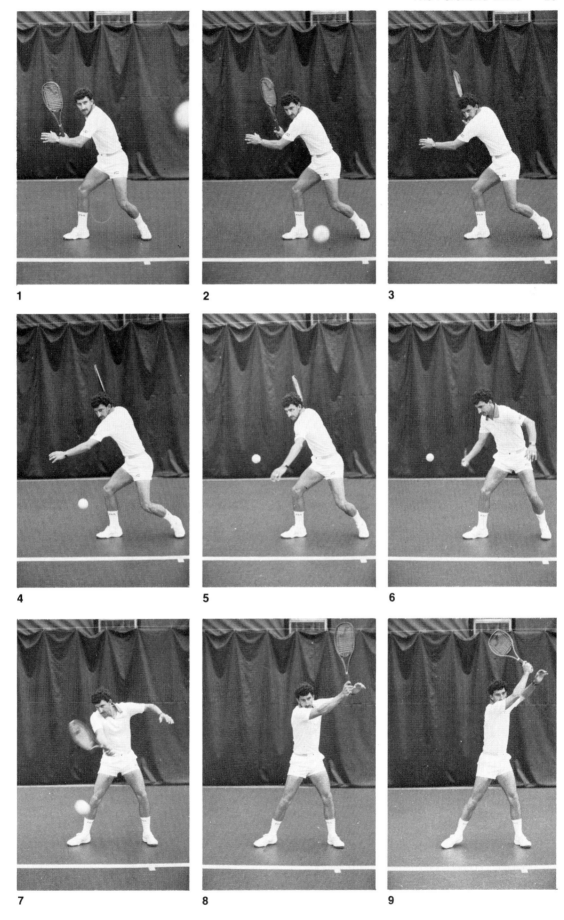

1

2

3

4

5

6

7

8

9

1   2   3   4

5   6   7   8

Here you can easily see how a topspin ground stroke is hit. The racket is swung from below the point of contact in a low-to-high motion.

Topspin

To hit a topspin forehand drive, you merely have to keep two things in mind. The forward swing must begin with the racket *below* where the point of impact will occur. As the racket is swung upward, the racket face must be near vertical as impact occurs, and the follow-through should continue upward. The more low-to-high your swing is, the greater the amount of topspin that can be produced on the ball. Notice how the player above swings the racket head to produce a

great deal of By hitting topspin on a tennis ball, the player is able to swing with a great amount of force. At the same time, the topspin causes a looping effect on the tennis ball, hopefully allowing it to stay within the court boundaries. Most follow-throughs are very exaggerated and have little effect on the outcome of the shot. For example, Steve Krulevitz uses a lot of topspin as you can see in the photographic sequences on page 25. However, in each case, his racket *must* be near vertical at contact.

1

In these two sequences, Steve Krulevitz shows the low-to-high action necessary for hitting topspin. Although his follow-through seems exaggerated, he must maintain a vertical racket face at impact.

2

3

1

2

3

Underspin

The other spin that a player can put on a tennis forehand drive is underspin. In placing underspin on the tennis ball, the player must do almost the opposite of what he did to hit topspin. That is, instead of the swing being from low-to-high, it must be from high-to-low. In addition, the racket may be slightly beveled backward to assist in propelling the ball over the net. Too much bevel, however, will cause the ball to float and send it beyond the court boundaries. In the photos below, observe how Vince Van Patten hits an exaggerated underspin forehand drive. The racket is taken back high and slightly laid back. As the forward swing begins, the racket is swung in a downward fashion toward ball impact. The racket is *slightly* beveled at impact, continues into the follow-through lower than the position of ball contact, and finishes up around the shoulders.

Vince Van Patten, winner of the 1981 Seiko Tournament, demonstrates how a forehand drive would be hit with excessive underspin.

1

2

3

4

4

The One-Handed Backhand Drive

Just as the forehand drive is considered by many to be the easiest stroke in the game, the one-handed backhand is probably the least appreciated stroke. It seems as though we are, time and time again, reminded of how weak our backhand is supposed to be. This is emphasized by the fact that our teachers and coaches tell us to attack our opponent's backhand in addition to telling us to spend time and effort working on our own. However, the one-handed backhand should not be that difficult a stroke to perform. In fact, movement of the upper arm using a one-handed backhand is much easier than swinging the arm forward across the trunk as you do in the forehand. Before describing the various performance characteristics of a good one-handed backhand, we need to analyze the most effective way of holding the racket.

ONE-HANDED BACKHAND GRIPS

The Continental Grip

Just as we described how to use the continental grip in hitting a forehand drive, the same grip can be used to hit a backhand; that's probably why it has the name continental. Most players who use a continental grip say they do not change grips; however, that is often not the case. In the photos at the top of page 28, observe a continental grip as used for a forehand drive. If you hit a backhand drive with that grip, look at the way you must hold your wrist. Most individuals who learn to play tennis with the continental grip usually shift the heel of the hand around to the right on the racket handle. Notice the lower sequence on page 28, which emphasizes this

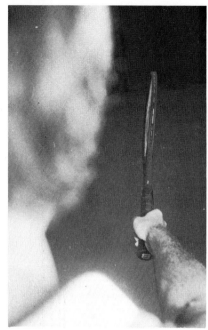

The continental grip as used for the forehand.

Notice the extreme tension placed on the wrist and forearm if you continually hit backhand drives with a continental grip.

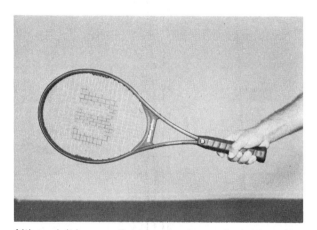

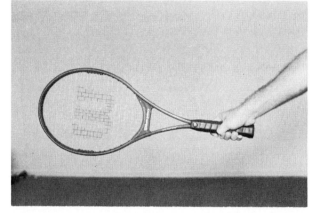

Although it is very slight, a grip change *is* employed by most players using the continental grip. Notice how the heel of the hand has slightly moved to accommodate the tension at the wrist.

slight grip change. The heel of the hand moves around to assist the swing of the racket. This change in grip, regardless of how slight it may seem, assists in accommodating the orientation of the wrist and also the force of impact. Nevertheless, a continental grip *can* be used effectively in the backhand drive. For example, John McEnroe uses a continental grip on his backhand drive and his backhand is not too bad! However, if you want consistency and don't want the problems of rotating the racket head into impact each time you swing, we advise you not to use the continental grip.

The Eastern Backhand Grip

The grip most commonly used for the one-handed backhand drive is the eastern backhand grip. Make the V with your swinging hand; then place your hand on the racket handle so that the base knuckle of your forefinger is directly on top of the flattened part of the racket. One way to

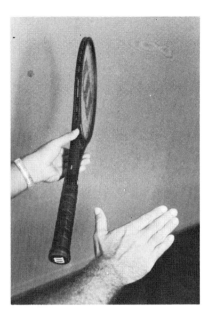

The hand orientation on the racket handle for the eastern backhand grip.

check if you have the racket held correctly is to place your arm directly out to the side as you hold the racket. This should orient the racket so that the racket head is vertical, as it would be when contacting the ball.

THE DRIVE

To hit a one-handed backhand drive, orient your body in the ready position in preparation for the stroke. (See page 30.) As soon as you are aware of the ball approaching your backhand, use the unit turn and take the racket back about shoulder height with the opposite hand holding the racket at the throat. As you begin to swing, drop the racket head *below* the level of ball contact and step toward the ball with the foot farthest from the ball. As you swing forward, swing the racket slightly upward and contact the ball about twelve to eighteen inches ahead of your front foot. The body weight transfer should be rhythmical with the swing; step, then swing. This allows for an optimum transfer of momentum and ensures firm ball contact.

Be sure to maintain the racket face as vertical as possible during impact. You should finish with a smooth, high follow-through.

In further analyzing an effective one-handed backhand, you should be aware of the various body parts that are used. As the rear foot gives a slight push off toward the front foot, there is an effective forward weight transfer. Notice how the hips rotate *slightly,* which, in turn, generates further rotation at the trunk. Then the upper arm comes into play and is accelerated through impact.

In essence, there are five body parts employed when you swing the racket forward with a one-handed motion: the ground reaction force is generated from the legs to the hips, through the trunk to the upper arm, the forearm, and finally to the hand and racket. Most tennis players have the ability to coordinate the leg, hip, and trunk action, transferring those forces out to the upper arm. However, coordinating the forearm action at the elbow and the hand action at the wrist creates problems for almost everyone learning the one-handed backhand. That's why so many players "lead with the elbow" or severely "drop the racket head" during a backhand drive. (See photos top of page 31.)

1   **2**   **3**

4   **5**   **6**

The proper mechanics to use when hitting a one-handed backhand drive. Observe the shoulder turn in preparation and also where contact occurs *ahead* of the body.

It's easy to see how problems can occur with stroke production when a player leads with the elbow.

SPIN

In addition to the utilization of five distinctly different body parts in striking a tennis ball, you should learn how to hit the backhand drive with various forms of spin to be the most effective tennis player possible.

Topspin

Topspin, at the early stages of development of the one-handed backhand drive, is extremely difficult. One reason may be that the muscles on the back side of the shoulder are a bit weaker than those on the front side, which are used for the forehand. Therefore, many people simply don't have the physical capabilities to accelerate the racket head in a low-to-high motion (remember what we said about hitting topspin for the forehand drive—it's the same for the backhand). In the photographs on page 32, you can see Butch Walts's topspin backhand. He must contact the ball with a vertical racket face far in front of his body and the racket must go through impact in a low-to-high fashion. It's for these strength-related reasons that many people do not hit tops-

pin backhands; they resort to an underspin backhand, a shot that's much easier to control.

Underspin

To hit a one-handed backhand drive with underspin, remember what was said about the forehand. As the author, Jack Groppel, demonstrates on page 33, the racket can be slightly open as it goes through the impact phase of the stroke and must be swung in a high-to-low fashion. Since the larger muscles in the middle-back region are used in this type of action, this movement is much easier to perform than a topspin backhand. On page 34, notice how Steve Krulevitz hits a one-handed backhand drive with underspin.

It may seem strange to you that many people find hitting a one-handed backhand to be so difficult. But perhaps that's why a majority of professional tennis instructors are currently starting all of their classes with lessons on the two-handed backhand. It seems to enable the students to hit more effectively at earlier stages of the game. Therefore, with that in mind, we need to examine the various characteristics of hitting a two-handed backhand drive.

1

2

3

4

Former U.S. Open quarter finalist Butch Walts illustrates his extremely effective topspin backhand.

1

2

3

4

5

6

Compare the body action of hitting an underspin backhand with that of the topspin backhand shown previously.

1

2

Steve Krulevitz demonstrates how a low, one-handed backhand can be hit effectively with underspin.

3

5

The Two-Handed Backhand Drive

Because of players like Chris Evert Lloyd, Jimmy Connors, Bjorn Borg, and Tracy Austin, the two-handed backhand has become incredibly popular. These players all began using a two-handed backhand early in the stages of their personal tennis development, probably because they didn't have adequate strength to control the racket when using a one-handed backhand. They also felt that topspin could be applied to the ball much more easily, and their effectiveness on the backhand side was greater through the use of two hands than if they only used a one-handed backhand.

With the increase in popularity of the two-handed backhand drive, it seems appropriate that we discuss exactly how highly skilled competitors use the stroke so effectively. First, we will begin with how you should grip the racket.

TWO-HANDED BACKHAND GRIPS

Two basic methods exist for holding the racket when using a two-handed backhand.

The Two Eastern Forehand Grips

The most commonly known method involves the use of two eastern forehand grips. Forming the V between your thumb and forefinger of your primary swinging hand, place it so that it is directly on top of the flattened portion of the racket handle. Then, make another V between the thumb and forefinger of your opposite hand and place it directly above your primary swinging hand so that the V of your opposite hand is also directly on top of the flattened portion of the racket handle. The photographs at the top of

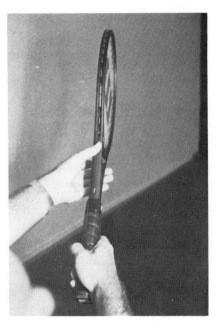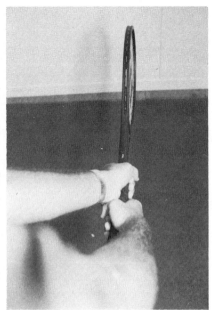

The proper grip techniques when using two eastern forehand grips for hitting a two-handed backhand drive.

this page show how the two hands should be placed when using two eastern forehand grips. Using this grip will make it easier to learn the backhand drive, because the beginning player doesn't have to bother changing grips as you would when using a one-handed backhand, going from an eastern forehand grip to an eastern backhand grip. However, one problem might exist for the player whose physical capabilities aren't up to what they should be to play the game of tennis. For example, we know that ball contact should occur slightly in front of the body. Notice the angle between the forearm and hand of this player's primary swinging hand. In trying to counter the force of impact with the wrist held at such an angle, much strain can be placed on

Observe how the right hand employs a continental grip, while the left hand is placed on the racket handle with an eastern forehand grip. This will ease the pressure placed on the wrist and forearm when hitting the two-handed backhand.

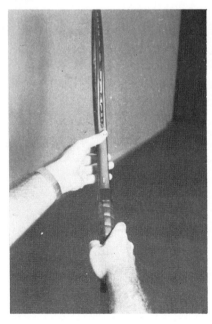

the muscles in the back part of the forearm. That's why many players do not use two eastern forehand grips for the two-handed backhand.

The Continental Grip

Instead, they use a continental grip for the primary swinging hand and an eastern forehand grip for the opposite hand. You can see from the photographs at the bottom of page 36 how the two grips are used, and note again the angle between the hand and forearm on the primary swinging hand. By moving to the continental grip, the player's forearm is more protected from the stress created by the wrist being held at an awkward angle.

Thus, if you wish to try a two-handed backhand, you might start with two eastern forehand grips. However, to prevent possible muscle strain, you should probably change at a later date to the continental grip for your primary swinging hand and an eastern forehand grip for your opposite hand.

THE DRIVE

Once you've selected the grip technique you feel most comfortable with, you're ready to hit a two-handed backhand. On page 38, notice how the ready position is employed by Mary Lou Piatek. The two hands are placed on the racket in very much the same way as if you were to use one hand. But instead of supporting the racket at the throat, the opposite hand is placed directly above the primary swinging hand. As soon as you see that your opponent's shot is headed toward the backhand side of your body, utilize the unit turn and prepare the racket for the swing by taking it back about head height. As the ball gets closer to you, drop the racket head below the point where you intend to hit the ball. As you are ready to swing, step toward the position of impact and swing the racket forward in a low-to-high motion, contacting the ball off the front foot. Your follow-through, using one of two common types, should be smooth and higher than the position of impact. The first type of follow-through is more of a straight-arm follow-through, like the one Mary Lou uses when involved in a baseline rally. The racket finishes high with the arms extended ahead of the body.

The second type of follow-through commonly used by highly skilled tennis players allows the elbows to flex, bringing the arms and racket up over the shoulders. Sue Arildsen demonstrates this technique by flexing her elbows after impact, causing the racket to "wrap" around her head and shoulders. (See page 39.)

Besides the fact that two hands are on the racket handle instead of one, there are many other ways of differentiating the two-handed from the one-handed backhand drive. For example, remember that the one-handed backhand effectively employs five distinctively different body parts in its motion. The two-handed backhand, in contrast, utilizes only two distinctly different body motions. As a player steps toward the ball for an effective weight transfer, the hips begin to rotate, followed quickly by the trunk and arms. In other words, the trunk and arms act as one body segment in bringing the racket around to impact. Following impact, however, the arms separate their motion from the trunk and can either use a straight-arm follow-through or a wrap follow-through. Since only two body parts are used in hitting a two-handed backhand, it is reasonable to assume that this would be an easier stroke to learn. This, in fact, is the case when we examine children learning a one-handed or two-handed backhand drive. They do seem to perform better at the early stages of development when they use a two-handed backhand.

SPIN

Topspin

As we mentioned earlier in this chapter, topspin is fairly easy to hit using two hands on the racket. Remember that we said topspin for the one-handed backhand is extremely difficult due to various strength factors. With two hands on the racket handle, you avoid the problems associated with strength, and most individuals can easily hit topspin with a two-handed backhand. The method of hitting the two-handed backhand with topspin is the same as with any other stroke; the motion must be low-to-high as Sue Arildsen, varsity tennis player at the University of Illinois, demonstrates on page 40, and the racket face must be nearly vertical at impact.

1

2

3

4

5

6

In this series of photographs, Mary Lou Piatek demonstrates the two-handed backhand that helped her gain
a top 20 world ranking.

7

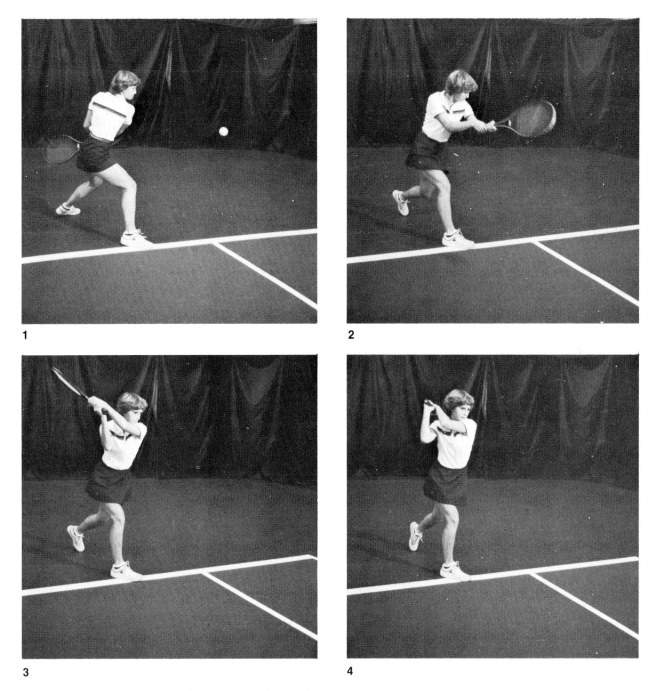

1

2

3

4

Sue Arildsen shows how the elbows can be allowed to flex and "wraps" the racket over her shoulder.

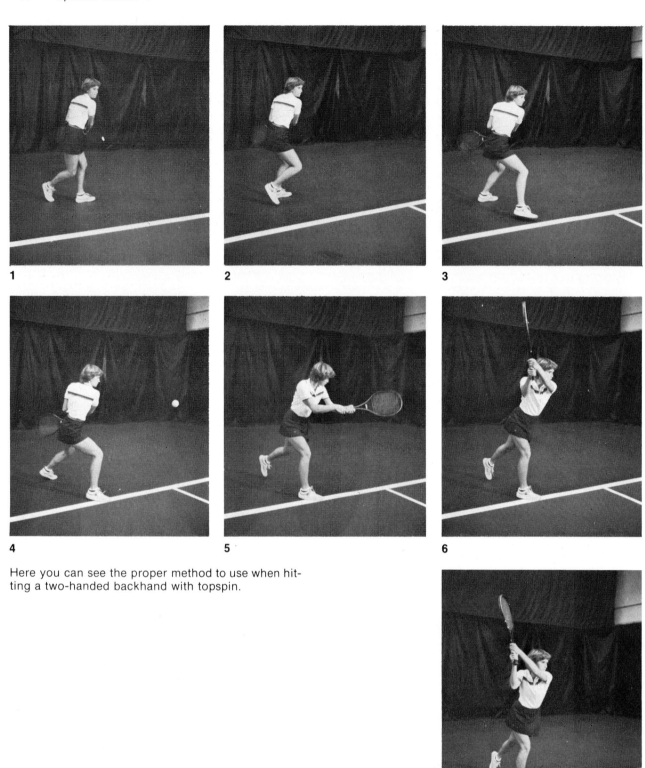

1

2

3

4

5

6

Here you can see the proper method to use when hitting a two-handed backhand with topspin.

7

1   2   3

Although slightly more difficult than hitting topspin, a two-handed backhand can be hit with underspin in the manner seen in these pictures. The racket must maintain a high-to-low pattern.

Underspin

Underspin, on the other hand, is *extremely difficult* to hit using two hands. This is due to the fact that the high-to-low motion with both hands on the racket handle causes a problem in terms of coordination. We previously discussed how the hip and trunk action can easily be employed for the low-to-high racket motion when hitting topspin, but when the high-to-low movement required for underspin is necessary, coordination is much more difficult. The hips and trunk, while bringing the racket forward, must also cause the racket to follow a downward trajectory. Obviously, it would be easier to swing forward and up for topspin than forward and down for underspin.

To hit a two-handed backhand with underspin, you must use a high-to-low swinging pattern through impact as the player on this page is attempting to do, and the racket can be slightly beveled as impact occurs.

4

5

ONE-HANDED VS. TWO-HANDED BACKHAND

Many people have said that the two-handed backhand should not be used due to its lack of reach, especially on shots that must be stretched for to hit the return. However, current research has shown that when a player is able to comfortably situate his or her body with respect to the ball, there is no difference in the distance of impact from the body between the one-handed and two-handed backhands. In reaction to the shot that has to be stretched for, we agree that a two-handed backhand probably could not be used effectively. Nevertheless, how many stretched-out, one-handed backhands have you seen hit offensively? In this situation, even the great competitors have to hit a defensive shot either as an underspin drive or as a lob. Our feeling is that a player who uses a two-handed backhand can easily learn this defensive one-handed backhand. Therefore, to avoid using a two-handed backhand because of its lack of reach seems ludicrous.

6

The Serve

Since the serve begins every point during a match, its importance to anyone playing the game of tennis is obvious. In this chapter, we will critically examine the various techniques required for an effective serve, starting with the service grip.

THE SERVICE GRIP

Depending upon the amount of spin you wish to hit on a serve—if any—you have a couple of grips to choose from. The service grip most commonly used is the continental grip, which has already been discussed. Usage of the continental grip enables the player to hit a very hard, flat serve or a serve with a great deal of spin. When pros desire to hit serves with extreme spin on the ball, they will often change their grips slightly so they use more of an eastern backhand grip. This grip does not allow the player to hit a very hard, flat serve, but will facilitate hitting the ball with spin.

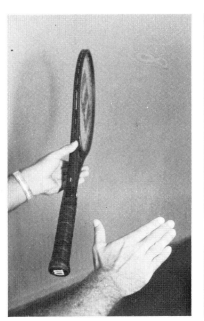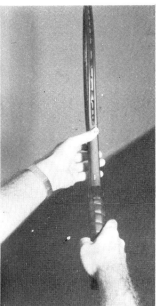

The continental grip recommended for serving.

Above, right, and next page: Notice the arm action of these professional tennis players when tossing the ball during their serve.

SERVICE MOTION

There are many important body parts involved in hitting an effective serve in tennis. People learning the game often have great difficulty hitting a good serve because they try to do too many things at once. Therefore, we will discuss what we feel are the most important elements of serving and then put them all together to form an efficient service motion for you. The first element to be discussed is the ball toss.

The Ball Toss

Just as the serve is the most important stroke in the game of tennis, the ball toss is probably the most important part of a good service motion. And it's amazing how many people don't know how to toss a ball correctly. We see all kinds of short, jerky, uneven actions. The key to a good toss is consistently putting the ball where it needs to be for impact. A good tossing action occurs from the shoulder with *very* little—if any—

movement at the wrist or elbow. A good cue to assist you in tossing the ball consistently is to think of "lifting" the ball into the air. Although some professional tennis players don't necessarily toss the ball vertically (they use sort of an arc when tossing, to facilitate their trunk action and also to propel the ball farther into the court), we suggest that you use a vertical toss to increase your consistency. You can see from the photographs on this page and page 45 how some of the top players move their arms to toss the ball. As a drill to test your own tossing consistency, toss the ball into the air about four to five feet; hold your hand still once the ball leaves it, and see if the ball comes right back down to your hand without having to move it.

Once you've achieved a consistent ball toss, how high should it go? This has been the subject of great controversy among many teaching authorities. Should the ball toss be higher than the point of impact? Should you try to hit the ball on the way up? Or should you try to hit the ball

when it's at its peak in the toss? Well, it would be ideal if you could hit the ball when it's at the peak of the toss because it is stationary at that point. However, that may be a bit idealistic. We suggest tossing the ball a bit higher than you can reach with your racket, as the majority of the pros do. This gives you ample time to go through the various motions required in swinging the racket and also provides you with a better way of estimating your timing.

Now, let's combine the toss with the swinging action. You can actually start a serve any way you wish. Many people like to stand at the base-line with the front foot at about a 45° angle to the baseline; the rear foot should be about shoulder-width distance apart from the front foot, and parallel to the baseline. Many players also like to start with the ball in the center of their racket, perhaps because this may be the only time the center of their racket ever sees the ball!

From this point, the tossing hand and the racket hand should move downward simultaneously. The racket should continue downward so it's almost pointing toward the ground and then begin an upward motion. Now, toss the ball by

1

2

3

4

5

6

Rick Vetter demonstrates the proper method to use when serving. It is important to recognize the transfer of force from the ground throughout his body to the racket.

7

lifting it into the air. *Remember* to keep the motion as fluid and simple as possible. Don't use extraneous or exaggerated motions when trying to hit an effective serve—simplest is probably the best. Once the ball is tossed, don't pull your tossing hand down too quickly. Keep it in the air as though you were aiming at the ball. By this point, the racket hand should have brought the racket up so the upper arm is almost at a right angle to the trunk. Now, your serve should resemble a throwing motion. If you can throw a ball, you can hit an effective serve. That's all you have to remember! Pretend you are going to "throw" the racket into the serve. Try to extend up as high as possible to ball contact and hit the ball straight out from the racket head. You shouldn't hit downward on a hard serve. Even Stan Smith, who is all of six feet, four inches and has an incredibly hard serve, can't hit downward very much on his serve. He hits straight out from the racket head.

Your follow-through should be across the body and uninterrupted by extraneous movements. The smoother your swing is, the better off you'll be.

Impact

Many people have difficulty in hitting the serve. Perhaps this is because so many different body motions must occur for the serve to be effective. Let's start at ground level and move all the way up to impact in analyzing an effective serve like Tim Gullikson's. (See page 48.) We will discuss all the body parts that are used, and where problems might occur in your swing. The first question is how do you generate an effective ground reaction force in hitting a serve?

Remember that much of the force in the game of tennis must come from the ground—this may be the most important part of serving. The only way for you to generate a ground reaction force is by bending and extending the knees. As you begin your downward motion of the racket hand and the tossing hand, bend the knees slightly. When you near the position where you are ready to swing forward, forcefully extend the knees toward the direction of impact. This motion will assist in initiating the ground reaction force, and a natural body weight transfer forward should

occur due to your leg extension toward the point of impact. Now, you are ready to swing the racket.

Earlier, we said that swinging the racket forward is just like throwing a ball. The throwing action causes the hips and trunk to rotate. This motion, in turn, transfers the ground reaction force (generated by extending the knees) into the hips and then to the trunk. As the trunk is rotating at a high velocity, the force is transferred out to the arm, which in turn transfers that force into the hand and racket.

The Wrist Snap

Movement of the wrist is extremely important in hitting an effective serve, simply because the wrist is the last body part used in relaying all of the force you've generated from the ground into the racket. Many people have used the term *wrist snap* in describing the action of the wrist. The wrist snap refers to several basic actions: flexion and extension of the wrist, sideways movements at the wrist, and pronation (rotation) of the hand and forearm. The actual occurrence of all these movements is the subject of great controversy among teaching pros. Some feel that *only* pronation of the hand and forearm occur and others feel that *each* joint action takes place during the forward swing. Current research, however, has shown that all three movements *do* occur when hitting an effective serve, making the term *wrist snap* a valid one.

Direction

Even though a wrist snap is proper to use when serving, many people still have problems in hitting the ball where they want it to go. One reason for this is that they don't understand the pronation that must occur in the forearm and hand. As you can see from the pictures of Mary Lou Piatek on page 49, the hand and racket head actually turn out after the ball has been hit. This action assists in transferring the ground reaction force through the body to the racket. If you can think of making impact with the palm facing the direction of your shot, it should help you to hit the ball where you want it to go.

1   2   3

4   5   6

Tim Gullikson, formerly ranked in the top 20 in the
world, illustrates the serve that got him to that level.
Watch how he seems to coil his body like a tight spring
and then uncoil it very quickly toward impact.

1

2

3

4

5

6

Mary Lou Piatek has one of the toughest serves in women's tennis. Notice how the force is transferred through the body, but especially be aware of the hand and racket pronating through impact.

7

These three professional tennis players demonstrate the position of the body as impact occurs in the tennis serve. It is important to remember, however, that none of these players consciously jump into their serve.

SERVICE TIPS AND TACTICS

The First Serve

You may be wondering by now what differences exist when hitting a first and second serve. Most of us know that the first serve is usually hit with a great deal more velocity than a second serve, and that it will place much less spin on the ball. The idea of a "cannonball" serve comes from the fact that a player will attempt to hit the first serve as hard as possible, yet with little spin. When hitting a hard first serve, skilled competitors will usually toss the ball far into the court toward the net and make their body the longest lever possible as they "reach" for a high impact. In extending the legs toward impact, you can see that most players actually lift themselves off the ground just before hitting the serve. None of these players consciously "jump" into their service motion. By forcefully extending their legs into the serve and transferring that force through the hips and trunk, they actually "pull" their body off the tennis court. So, don't try to consciously jump into a serve. Merely make your body the longest lever possible and extend yourself up into the ball at impact. Remember, how-

ever, that no matter how hard you hit the ball, you can't hit downward very much into the court; the ball must be hit straight out from the racket head.

The Second Serve

When hitting a second serve, don't take many chances because you only have this last chance to get the ball into the service court before losing the point. Therefore, you will have to take a bit of velocity off the stroke and place more spin on the ball to increase the likelihood of hitting a good serve. As Butch Walts demonstrates on the next page, to hit the ball with more spin and yet with an optimum velocity, the ball should not be tossed as far into the court as you did on your hard, flat first serve. The ball will usually be tossed a bit more overhead and your back may be slightly arched (although this back motion may *not* be suitable for many people because of the possibility of back injury). The racket head must be accelerated in a low-to-high fashion through impact, brushing the back of the ball to produce the type of spin desired. Hitting the ball to produce various spins can be related to the face of a clock. When you toss the ball straight

1

2

3

4

5

6

Butch Walts is said to have one of the toughest serves
in tennis. Here you can witness his second serve.

upward, imagine that the top of the ball is twelve o'clock on the dial. If you wish to hit a slice serve (one with a great deal of sidespin), the ball must be hit in a three o'clock fashion. If you desire to hit a serve that will "kick" up when it bounces, you need to hit a twelve o'clock or a one o'clock type of spin. We recommend that if you wish to hit a good spin serve, begin by hitting a sidespin serve (one that is hit with a three o'clock motion), because the other movements can cause some trauma to your lower back if you are inexperienced at hitting spin serves.

7

The Volley

Although many people are happy staying at the baseline hitting ground strokes all day long, others feel they can take the offensive much more readily against their opponent if they can get to the net and hit volleys. The volley, however, is difficult for many people, possibly because they are no longer more than eighty feet away from their opponent, and because the ball doesn't get a chance to slow down from its bounce toward them. When players approach the net, they are usually no more than fifty feet away from the opponent, and a decision must quickly be made on how and where to volley the ball as it approaches them in flight. This creates a great deal of fear in many tennis players, regardless of their skill level. Therefore, the first thing you need to do is stop being afraid of the net. You can even think of your racket as a weapon you could use to protect yourself! Once you've decided that it won't hurt very long, even if the ball *does* hit you, you're ready to learn the volley!

GRIP TECHNIQUE

How to properly hold the racket when volleying has been a controversial topic in recent years. Two trains of thought exist about which grip is most effective: (1) change grips from an eastern forehand grip for the forehand volley to an eastern backhand grip for the backhand volley; or (2) use a continental grip for both volleys. The rationale for changing grips when volleying is that both the eastern forehand grip and eastern backhand grip maintain a vertical racket face. In contrast, the continental grip allows the racket face to be slightly open, which assists the player in clearing the net on low volleys. It also helps in placing a slight amount of underspin on the ball, hopefully facilitating control of the volley.

The biggest argument heard against changing grips is, "I simply don't have enough time to change grips when I'm in a real fast volley war at the net during my weekly doubles!" Realistically,

The volley is an extremely important part of tennis.   Ross Case, one of the world's premiere doubles players, shows how to hit an aggressive volley.

now, how often are you in those "real fast" volley situations at the net where all four players are viciously slamming the ball at one another? Therefore, avoiding the grip change technique of volleying simply because of time limitation seems to be a poor reason. The continental grip, on the other hand, is also good to use except when hitting down the line volleys. Imagine yourself at the net in the center of the court and a ball has been hit to your forehand. To volley the return down the line, the hand must move in an inside-out motion to hit the necessary angle. This can cause serious problems with control in many tennis players. It is our recommendation that you use the eastern grip change method in volleying,

especially in the early stages of learning it. Then, if you wish, you can change to the continental method.

THE VOLLEY

Now that you've decided which grip technique you're going to use when you get to the net, let's discuss how you're going to hit the ball. There are actually two ways of hitting an effective volley: (1) the punch volley and (2) the drive volley.

The Punch Volley

The punch volley is a very short stroke which

To avoid situations such as this, try to keep your racket well ahead of your body. That will minimize the possibility of getting hit.

Rick Vetter illustrates the movements necessary to hit a punch volley. It is important that the racket go forward, ahead of the body, as quickly as possible.

aims for control, yet with not as much velocity as a drive volley. The racket is usually held in front of the body and the first movement should be forward toward the point of impact. It is a well-timed maneuver which can be very effective (sometimes more effective than attempting a drive volley).

The Drive Volley

The drive volley, on the other hand, involves more of a swinging motion. The racket may be brought back in almost a full backswing and then swung forward to contact the ball in front of the body.

The drive volley, in contrast to the punch volley, involves a much longer stroke. Notice here how the backswing is used to generate a higher racket velocity.

Although this manner of volley footwork isn't really recommended, it is sufficient as long as the ball is coming right to you.

Most of our problems in volleying occur when we try to imitate a great volleyer like John McEnroe (who utilizes a drive volley very often), because we simply do not have the timing that McEnroe does. Most players who try a drive volley when they are not that experienced usually end up hitting the ball into the fence on a fly! The drive volley, if attempted too soon in the development of a good volley, can cause more problems than it can help. Therefore, until you become skilled at volleying, it is recommended that you use the punch method of volleying.

1

Rick Vetter shows us how to hit a side-step volley. This can be used when the ball is slightly farther to the side.

2

3

1

Here you can see the crossover step volley. This type of footwork gives you the greatest range of motion and is most often recommended when you have time to do it.

2

3

The block volley must be used when the ball is coming right at you. It is much more easily hit when using a backhand volley as you see here.

1 2

3 4

As you can see here, the two-handed volley can be very effective *if* the ball is coming right to you. It can create problems, however, if you have to stretch.

Footwork

Various forms of footwork exist in hitting an effective volley.

The first is obviously the simplest since it requires *no* footwork. In hitting this type of volley, the ball naturally comes very close to you and all you have to do is swing the racket. This may seem like a very lazy manner of volleying, but it can be quite effective *only* if the ball is coming right to you. (See top of page 56.)

A second type is the side step volley (page 56), where the foot on the side toward which the ball is heading simply moves slightly to that side, transferring weight in that direction, and contact is made ahead of the body.

The third and most highly recommended type is the crossover step volley. This creates an effective transfer of weight toward the position of impact and gives the volleyer the greatest range of motion. (See top of page 57.)

Finally, you may be in a situation where the ball is coming right at you. Don't panic! Simply hold the racket as though you were going to hit a backhand volley, and move the racket toward the ball as it approaches your body. This is called a block volley. (See bottom of page 57.)

The Two-Handed Volley

Many people don't like to hit a one-handed backhand volley because they feel that they don't have the strength to control the racket. In a situation like this, they often resort to a two-handed volley. (See photos above.) This stroke is acceptable as long as the players aren't planning to get into competitive tennis. You may recall our saying that when you hit ground strokes using a two-handed backhand, you still have plenty of time to stretch out and hit the defensive return as a lob or underspin shot. Well, the same is *not*

Here you can see some of the problems a net player runs into if only a two-handed volley is used.

true for volleying. When you are at the net, you are in a very offensive and strategic position and cannot afford to play defensive tennis. When the ball is hit to the backhand side of your body and your reach is limited with a two-handed stroke, you will invariably lose the point if you're playing a skilled competitor. Mary Lou Piatek (pages 60 and 61), for example, uses a two-handed volley when the ball is close but she also has an excellent one-handed volley when she needs it.

If you lack the strength necessary to hit a good backhand volley with one hand, then you should resort to two hands. Hopefully, as your skill in tennis develops, you will be able to change to a one-handed stroke which will give you the little bit better reach required during those quick actions at the net.

Dishing the Racket Face

What about all the racket movement we see the pros make when they volley a ball? They seem to actually turn the racket under the ball at impact. This "dishing" of the racket has created great controversy among teachers and it's understandable why problems exist with explaining what really happens. As Steve Krulevitz volleys (page 62), the racket *seems* to move under and around the ball, thereby helping to place underspin on the ball. Observe the higher-speed sequence photography on page 63 to see what really occurs. Notice that the player has a firm racket face through impact and that no deviation of the racket head occurs *until* the ball has been hit. Therefore, the motion of the racket head as it dishes has absolutely no effect on the ball. The

dishing effect is the result of the racket's reaction to impact with the tennis ball. In addition, it is not recommended that you try this dishing action merely because someone else does it. First, you are not transferring optimum momentum to the ball at impact when the racket reacts like this, and second, you'll probably dish too soon and lose total control of the shot.

Hitting Deep

When you see highly skilled tennis players at the net, you will notice that few volleys are intentionally hit short into the court. As we've said before, the strategy behind volleying is to gain the most offensive position possible by increasing the amount of court available for you to hit into. Practice hitting deep into the opponent's court to keep him or her off balance during a point. If you hit short into the court and the opponent is able to get to the ball, you could easily lose the point. You should also practice hitting the ball straight out from the racket head—*never* hit down. Notice the ball leaving the player's racket on page 63; it's directed straight out and not down. If you hit downward when volleying, you only increase the likelihood of losing the point.

High/Low Volleys

What about different forms of volleying when the ball is high and when the ball is low? On high volleys, everything is the same. You should use very little backswing and the ball should be hit straight out from the racket head. This form may

1

2

Mary Lou Piatek has a very good two-handed volley. However, if the ball is low, as shown here, or if she must stretch to the side (next page), she is also capable of hitting a good one-handed volley.

3

1

2

3

1

2

3

As Steve Krulevitz hits a one-handed backhand volley, notice what happens as soon as the ball is hit. The racket seems to move under and around the ball in a "dishing" fashion. As we know, that dishing has *no* effect on the ball.

Observe the proper form in hitting a volley. The racket face stays firm *until* the ball has left the racket. Although you should try to keep the racket face firm, it is not always possible.

Rick Vetter demonstrates how the ball should be hit from the racket face. Notice that the ball is not hit in a downward direction, but straight out from the racket face.

1

When hitting a high volley, use very little backswing and contact the ball in front of your body, hitting it deep into the court.

2

3

Butch Walts shows how low a player often must get to hit an effective low volley.

seem a bit questionable since the ball is so much higher than the net. However, if you hit downward on a high volley, you will usually hit too short into the court and the opponent will easily be able to get to the ball and have a good chance of winning the point. On low volleys, you must think of one very important factor: getting your "seat" as low as possible to the ground. This will make it easier for the racket to get beneath the ball and propel it over the net. The racket face will also have to be slightly open to help the ball clear the net. Very little backswing should occur in a low volley, and a short stroke should be used in hitting the ball as deep into the opponent's court as possible.

Remember, volleying is intended to be an aggressive maneuver, placing you in a strategically advantageous position. If you try to play offensively when at the net, you should be able to improve your game tremendously.

Laura Dupont demonstrates the proper method for hitting a low forehand volley. Notice how far in front of her body contact will occur.

8

How to Get to the Net

Even though you may already know how to hit an extremely effective volley, it will do you little good unless you know how to get to the net to use your volley. Two methods exist that will provide you with a means for getting there. The first and possibly the most common is the serve and volley.

THE SERVE AND VOLLEY

You can see in the photographs on pages 68–69 how this player attempts the serve and volley. Once the ball has been hit, the server's trail leg continues around and he begins striding toward the net. Notice how, when he feels it's time to prepare for the volley, he discontinues his striding pattern and separates his feet to plant them a little more than shoulder width apart and almost parallel to the net. This "split step" makes his body momentarily stable and balanced. Al-

though it occurs very quickly and only lasts a fraction of a second, this split step enables the player to be adequately prepared for hitting the first volley. Depending upon how quick a tennis player is in approaching the net, the first volley is usually hit somewhere near the service line. Just as we discussed in the previous chapter, notice that the first volley is hit with the knees flexed and the eyes low, near the ball level. Once the first volley has been hit, the tennis player needs to "close in" toward the net in preparation for the second volley. The player should continue to close in until he or she is about eight to ten feet from the net so that any short ball hit by the opponent can be returned with a winner. Any closer than eight to ten feet to the net, and our tennis player becomes vulnerable to a lob from the opponent.

A couple of points are very important to make here. One is that the first volley should seldom be

In this series of pictures, Rick Vetter demonstrates the proper method for the serve and volley maneuver. Observe how the rear leg in the serve actually goes right into a complete stride as he hits the ball. Then, notice how he split steps in preparation for volleying.

7

8

9

10

11

12

A good serve and volley is a definite necessity when playing doubles. Notice how the player serves the ball and then approaches the net so he maintains a position near his partner. This makes the serving team very offensive since they are usually about ten feet from the net and can hit aggressive volleys into the opponents' court.

1

2

3

4

5

6

7

8

9

10

11

12

13

14

15

1

Right and next page: When the ball is hit short into his court, Rick Vetter shows how to hit the approach shot down the line. Notice that he doesn't really stop to hit the ball but instead maintains his balance and moves through the stroke.

hit for a winner. The player hitting the first volley is simply too deep into his own court to attempt hitting such an aggressive shot. Instead, the first volley should be hit so it places the opponent in a defensive position and allows a winner to be hit on the second or third volley. The second point to remember is that stability and balance are extremely necessary when performing a serve and volley. Once you go into the split step, you commit yourself to preparing for the opponent's return. If you are off-balance or if you continue running through your first volley, the results of the shot will obviously be poor.

Let's take a look at how a serve and volley can be used in doubles. From the rear view shown in the pictures on pages 70–71, you can see the player serve and approach the net adjacent to his partner. Once the opponent begins to swing forward to hit the return of serve, the server split steps in preparation for the first volley. If the server split steps sooner than this, it places him too far back into his own court. Along the same lines, if the server continues running toward the net, he may be caught in a very unbalanced situation for hitting the first volley. That's why the timing involved in using a serve and volley is most important. Since a good serve and volley are necessary in skilled doubles, you should learn when to split step and how to maintain your balance in volleying. From the balanced position, you then need to learn how to have your body weight move forward to hit the most effective volley possible, as we discussed in the last chapter.

In singles, however, you may not feel comfortable attempting a serve and volley due to various reasons. For example, your serve may not be the best possible or you may feel uncomfortable running toward the net following your serve. In a case like this, you still may realize the importance of getting to the net and will need to learn how to take advantage of situations when the opponent mistakenly hits a ball short into your court. This requires the use of an approach shot, which you will follow to the net in preparing to volley.

THE APPROACH SHOT

When the opponent hits short into your court (for example, near your own service line), you may wish to "approach" the net. In hitting an approach shot, you can see from the photograph above and those on the next page that you don't necessarily need total stability for the shot. By that we mean that you don't have to actually stop to hit an approach shot, but instead can continue your forward movement as long as you are balanced. But in moving through the shot, you *must* stay well-balanced. You can't allow any extraneous body movements that will cause your shot to be errant.

Once you recognize that the opponent has hit a ball short enough so that you feel comfortable hitting an approach shot, you should begin moving toward the ball as Mary Lou Piatek demonstrates on page 74. If at all possible, don't let the ball drop too low. Try to get your body to the

2

3

4

5

6

7

court position where impact will occur at about waist or chest level. By doing so, you will be able to maintain much better control over your upper body when swinging to hit the ball. As you begin to move through the approach shot, be sure the racket is back and your body is slightly sideways to the net. Many people try to hit an open-stance approach shot and tend to lose total control of the shot. Once you get near the impact position, begin your forward swing as you continue to move through the shot and maintain your balance. Impact should occur slightly ahead of your body and your follow-through should continue along the ball's flight path. Two rules of thumb exist when hitting an approach shot. First of all, you should usually approach down the line. As the author, Jack Groppel, demonstrates on page 75, you can see how a down the line approach should look. He keeps his body sideways to the net even though he's been forced to hit a low approach shot. However, on page 76, you can see

Mary Lou Piatek shows how to hit an underspin approach shot. Notice the high-to-low racket motion and also the intense concentration on the ball.

1

2

3

what happens when a player tends to approach crosscourt and leaves the opposite sideline wide open for the opponent's passing shot.

The second point of importance concerns how you should hit the ball. In general, when the ball is above the height of the net, you can hit flat or with slight topspin. When the ball is contacted below the height of the net's tape, you should usually put underspin on the ball. When hitting the underspin approach shot, try to keep the ball low, yet deep into the opponent's court. If you loft the ball into the air with underspin, the ball will bounce more vertically and allow the opponent an easy passing shot. In contrast, some players will hit a high, looping approach shot when they get the short ball around chest level.

Here you see the author, Jack Groppel, hitting an approach shot down the line. Notice how his body is sideways to the net, which facilitates the down the line stroke.

1

2

3

4

Although this shot requires a great deal of skill, it forces the opponent to attempt a passing shot or a defensive lob about head level on his or her own body.

In summary, when you hit the ball deep to the opponent on an approach shot, he won't have the opportunity to make an easy short shot to pass you with when you're at the net. Also, by keeping the approach shot as low as possible, you force the opponent to hit "up" on the ball in attempting to clear the net during his passing shot. This can create numerous control problems for your opponents, and it will make your own game more effective.

The crosscourt approach shot should be avoided unless you intend it to be a winner. Here we can see Fred Marchese hitting a crosscourt approach shot. Notice Fred's position after he hits the ball as well as the position of his opponent. Fred, a teaching pro, has left the opponent with an easy down the line passing shot for a winner.

1

2

3

4

5

6

7

9

The Return of Serve

Just as the serve is the most important stroke in the game of tennis because it begins every point of a match, the return of serve is equally important for the opponent. Anyone who has played tennis or watches it on television knows how important it is to "break" someone's serve (which means to win the game when the opponent is serving). Interestingly enough, while many people work diligently on developing their service motion, few people really work on manicuring their return of serve. It's these people who end up losing close matches because they can seldom break the opponent's serve. Therefore, it will benefit you to understand the most efficient way to return serve as well as how you can use an effective service return to take the offensive against your opponent.

A good return of serve begins with a ready position, which already has been described. When returning serve, you should decide the two most extreme places in the service box where the opponent could hit the ball. Usually, you should assume he can hit the T formed by the service

Notice the court position of Sandy Collins as she prepares to return serve.

Right and next page: Mary Lou Piatek illustrates the service return that helped her achieve her world class status. Watch how she employs the unit turn and synchronizes her footwork with her body movement.

1

line and center service line and that he can hit the singles sideline about halfway along the service box. You should then position yourself so you bisect the angle created by these potential serves. It's for this reason that you see most pros line up near the singles sideline at the baseline; they are bisecting the angle of their opponent's serve possibilities.

THE UNIT TURN

Once you've determined where to stand while receiving your opponent's serve, your preparation involves going from your own ready position into the unit turn. For example, if you see that the serve is traveling toward your backhand, you should perform the unit turn as shown by Mary Lou Piatek above and on the next page. With the unit turn, the racket goes into its full backswing position. At this point, you can do one of two things: hit a flat (or slight topspin) return as Mary Lou has done, or hit a "chip" return (one with underspin).

THE TOPSPIN RETURN

To hit the flat or topspin return, the racket must be taken back and dropped lower than the position of impact. This enables you to swing in a low-to-high fashion and the follow-through

should continue in that upward direction. If you use the proper timing, this should permit you to hit the return with the type of spin you desire. Remember, as we discussed before, the more low-to-high you swing the racket, the more topspin you will gain. However, a serve is often traveling at such a rate that a vast amount of topspin is quite difficult, even with the two-handed backhand. Therefore, we suggest that you try to hit the return as flat as possible or even use a simpler method: the underspin service return.

THE UNDERSPIN RETURN

In hitting an underspin return of serve, the racket must be taken back higher than the point of impact. As the author, Jack Groppel, demonstrates on page 80, the forward swing must be in a high-to-low fashion with the racket being slightly beveled at impact. The combination of these two factors allows the ball to be hit with underspin and also to be projected from the racket so it will clear the net. The underspin return of serve usually allows the player more control, since a shorter backswing may be used and the timing required is not quite as crucial as when hitting flat or with topspin. However, when you use the underspin return of serve for its added control, you should realize that you are giving up the advantage of the high velocity you

2 3 4

5 6 7

may receive from hitting a flat or topspin return. Most of you, however, should not be too concerned with a forceful return at this point. We suggest that you work on your timing in hitting an effective return of serve with underspin.

THE LOB

Another type of return often seen in doubles competitions is the lob. On page 81, notice how this player in a doubles game hits the lob return of serve. First, the racket is taken back slightly lower than the point of impact. Then, as the racket approaches the point of contact, it is beveled quite a bit to project the ball in an upward manner so it will clear the reach of the net person on the other side. The follow-through is high, yet smooth and controlled, and not hit with a great

1

2

3

4

The author demonstrates an effective underspin return of serve. Here you can see the high-to-low racket movement and the slight bevel of the racket head at impact.

The lob return of serve is extremely effective in the game of doubles. Here, Rick Vetter demonstrates how the racket must travel in a low-to-high fashion with an extreme bevel so the ball will be hit upward over the head of the net person on the opposite court.

1

2

3

4

5

1

The footwork on the return of serve is extremely important. Observe how a slight hop takes place prior to the unit turn. This hop "sets" the muscles of the legs, preparing them to thrust in the direction of the serve.

2

3

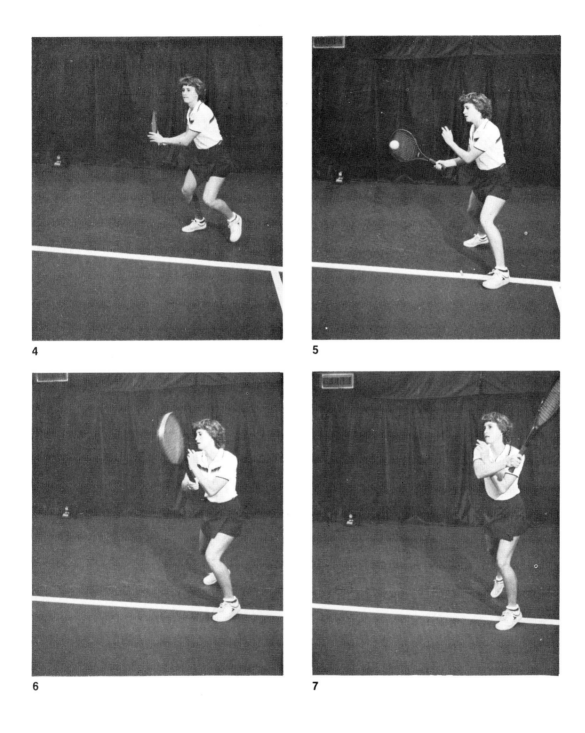

4

5

6

7

deal of velocity. Remember, when hitting the lob return of serve, you are working on control to hit the ball deep and over the reach of the opposing net person.

FOOTWORK

One area we need to cover more thoroughly on the service return is footwork. Often, you will see professional tennis players take a slight hop prior to hitting their return, and the hop is usually forward into the court. This hop, as we mentioned in an earlier chapter, places the muscles in a set position and allows for quick movements in any direction. The movement forward facilitates the unit turn movement. In other words, as the player moves forward with a short hop into the court, and the unit turn takes place, the player is slightly off-balance forward into the court. You should understand, at this point, that many serves are of such high velocity that the traditional "step into the shot" form is impossible.

Therefore, highly skilled players do the next best thing. By taking the short hop into the court and immediately performing the unit turn, they are slightly off-balance forward, which facilitates the transfer of linear momentum into the shot. This type of movement requires very good timing to determine when you should take the hop, when to perform the unit turn, and how to control your body. The photographs on pages 82-83 of Sue Arildsen performing this movement should be of some assistance to you. However, to understand the necessary timing involved, you must practice this yourself against players who serve with different velocities. That's the only way you will learn your own personal rhythm of taking the short hop and moving into your return of serve. The main thing to avoid is hopping high off the court. Remember, the goal of this movement is to move forward, not upward. If you move too high upward, you decrease your forward momentum and can severely hamper your return of serve.

10

The Lob and Overhead Smash

THE LOB

One of the most misunderstood shots in the game of tennis is the lob. For some unknown reason, many contemporary players don't understand how an effective lob can benefit their game. Perhaps these players feel that lobbing is not an aggressive form of tennis. However, any of you who feel that way should watch what happens when professional tennis players go to the net. In doubles, especially, you will see numerous lobs used to get the opponents away from their net positions. Lobbing, when employed in this manner, can be much more beneficial than trying to ram a ground stroke down your opponent's throat. And, as far as technique is concerned, it takes more skill to hit a good lob—one that has enough height to clear the opponent's reach, yet is deep enough into the opponent's court to allow you to take the advantage.

The Defensive Lob

The lob most commonly used is the defensive lob. A player hits this shot when there is no other alternative but to send the ball up into the air. This lob is sent fairly high into the air and as deep as possible into the opponent's back court. The purpose of the shot's height is to give a player ample time to regain an optimum court position. The purpose of hitting deep into the opponent's court is to force the opponent as far back into his or her own court as possible. The defensive lob is incredibly effective as a return of serve in doubles and also when the opponent or opponents (in doubles) are in an advantageous position at the net.

The defensive lob is hit in the manner illustrated on page 86. The racket is taken back *slightly* lower than the point of impact. The racket face should be quite open to facilitate an upward projection of the ball following impact.

1   2

3   4

Rick Vetter demonstrates how to hit the defensive lob. The racket is swung in a low-to-high fashion with a beveled racket face at impact. A slight underspin should be placed on the ball when hitting a defensive lob.

The racket should be swung forward in a low-to-high manner, and the open racket face should hit the ball with slight underspin. This underspin helps to keep the ball in the air longer and will also allow you to hit with more control. The added control gained from hitting underspin should enable you to clear your opponent's racket and get the ball deep into his or her court to gain an offensive position.

The Offensive Lob

The second type of lob frequently used is the offensive lob. In this type of shot, disguise is extremely necessary. The opponent is usually at a position near the net and is ready to volley your ground stroke. The idea is to make the opponent think that you are going to hit a ground stroke and, at the last minute, send the ball just high enough to clear his or her racket and yet land within the court boundaries. The element of surprise and the way you hit the ball make this stroke a very useful weapon in your repertoire of shots.

To hit an offensive lob, everything in terms of preparation should be the same as though you were hitting a normal ground stroke. You can see how the player at the top of the next page performs the unit turn and takes the racket back as he normally would for a ground stroke. Yet, at the last instant, he accelerates the racket head in an *extreme* low-to-high fashion (sometimes, the racket face will be *slightly* open at contact), attempting to project the ball just over the oppo-

The offensive lob, considered to be a real crowd pleaser, employs an extreme low-to-high racket movement but usually places a great amount of topspin on the ball.

nent's reach. The ball is hit with enough topspin so that when it lands it will take off and bounce away from the opponent as he or she tries to run it down. Needless to say, the timing required for this type of shot is crucial. However, if you can hit topspin ground strokes from baseline to baseline, simply try to clear the net by fifteen or twenty feet and yet make the ball land in the opponent's court. If you can accomplish this, you *can* hit an offensive topspin lob. Not only will it be an effective weapon, but you'll be the talk of the town once you can hit it consistently.

We've all heard the familiar expression, "What goes up must come down." This also applies to a lob. When your opponent has hit a lob and you are able to return the shot, you will probably want to return it in the most aggressive manner possible—with an overhead smash.

THE OVERHEAD SMASH

There are two ways of preparing to hit an effective overhead: to be completely stable and remain in contact with the ground, or to reach a greater height by jumping off the rear foot as you initiate the swing.

The Standing Overhead

Whenever you get the opportunity to hit an overhead smash, remember that stability is of prime importance. If at all possible, *stay on your feet.* Hitting an overhead is just like hitting a serve. You must turn your body sideways to the net and have your feet about shoulder width apart. When you are ready to hit the ball, swing forward, thinking of the same cues we discussed in explaining a serve. Hold up your opposite hand as though you have just tossed the ball on your serve. This will assist you in aiming toward the point of impact. Then, as you are ready to swing, simply move the racket through your normal throwing pattern. Hitting an overhead—just like hitting a serve—is similar to throwing a ball. The point of impact should occur slightly ahead of the body, and then you should allow the racket to come across your body and down toward your legs in a complete follow-through.

Many people have a hard time determining how to line up their bodies relative to the ball when it has been hit high into the air. First of all, if you are just learning to hit an overhead, *let it bounce.* This allows you to track the ball up as the opponent hits it; track the ball down as it approaches the court; track it back upward as it bounces from your court; and finally continue tracking it toward your own body. As it completes its downward path toward your body, line up as though the ball would hit you directly in the chest if it were allowed to fall. This forces you to hit the ball slightly ahead of your body. Those of you who are more advanced should probably

1

2

3

4

Rick Vetter demonstrates how to achieve total stability by maintaining contact with the ground. His overhead motion resembles that of a serve as he transfers his weight from rear foot to front foot and uses hip and trunk rotation to accelerate the racket.

Ann White, another world-class competitor, realizes the time factor involved in hitting an overhead smash prior to the ball bouncing. Here you see Ann contacting the ball well in front of her body to hit the effective overhead.

learn to hit the ball before it bounces, as Ann White demonstrates above. Although it is necessary to let the ball bounce at the early stages of learning the overhead, when you play highly skilled tennis, the bounce only allows your opponent more time to get set and attempt to read your next shot. However, you should realize that it's more difficult to hit an overhead smash before the ball bounces. When you let the ball bounce to hit the overhead, you can follow it upward from the opponent's racket, down to the ground, up again, and then down toward your body. When you hit it before it bounces, you can only watch it go up off the opponent's racket before it immediately heads downward toward you. The timing and depth perception required are a bit greater than when you allow it to bounce upward and then strike it on its way down. Again, however, you should line up the flight path of the ball so that it would strike you in the chest if it were allowed to come all the way

to your body. This will not only help you to hit an effective overhead from a strategic point of view, but will also force you to hit it so you don't get hit yourself! Sometimes, however, your opponent will hit a lob that makes it impossible for you to position your body under the flight path of the ball; yet, you may be able to hit an effective overhead if you can leave the ground as you can see Sue Arildsen doing on the next page.

The Jump Overhead

Hitting a jump overhead is actually not a very difficult maneuver. It only requires a considerable amount of timing which can be learned through practice. In hitting the jump overhead, you must turn your body sideways as you initiate the motion and, depending upon how you time your maneuver, jump a bit backward and upward so you can keep the ball in front of your upper body. Use your opposite hand and point

1

2

3

4

In competition, it is often impossible to hit an overhead smash and be completely stable. As Sue Arildsen illustrates, to hit the jump overhead you must leave the ground from the rear foot, rotating the body to accelerate the racket head through impact.

Notice how Mary Lou Piatek has her left arm in the air, almost pointing toward the ball. Her body is turned sideways to the net, and then she rotates her hips and upper body to bring the racket effectively toward impact.

toward the position of impact, directing your aim. Even though you are off the ground, swing as though you are throwing a ball. This throwing action, regardless of your position in the air, is still very important in allowing your hips and trunk to generate a high arm velocity. You should have full arm extension to reach as high as possible, giving you the greatest leverage on your overhead smash. The follow-through on a jump overhead is identical to that of the standing overhead. You should follow through across your trunk and downward so the racket finishes down around your legs.

Velocity and Direction

One final point to discuss is how the ball should be hit. Two very important factors come to mind. One is the velocity of the shot, and the other is the direction of the shot. The speed of an overhead smash is often devastating among pro-

fessional tennis players. However, once you learn to hit an effective overhead, you will learn that velocity is not alone in importance. Control should be just as important to you as high velocity. Therefore, when practicing your overhead, hit the ball to various corners but with not so much velocity that you impede your control. The angle of an overhead ball hit correctly off the racket face is a very interesting phenomenon. When you contact an overhead, you feel that you are very high above the net and that you *must* hit downward. This is definitely not the case! You should never think of hitting downward on an overhead smash unless you are right by the net and wish to bounce the ball over the back fence. Most often, you should attempt to hit the ball straight out from the racket face and work on hitting your overhead with depth into the opponent's court. You will have a much more effective and also a more penetrating overhead, making it a more useful weapon.

11

The Risky Shots: Drop Shot, Drop Volley, and Half-Volley

What do we mean by risky shots? Although you've seen the game's great players hit fantastic drop shots from anywhere on the court, these shots are usually low percentage attempts by anyone who is not an advanced player. Players use them because of the appreciation they receive from a crowd and also because they make their opponents look humble. At one time or another, we've all dreamt of hitting hard ground strokes from corner to corner and watching the opponent sprint to return each ball, only to have us hit a drop shot that is literally rolling by the time it gets to the opponent's service line. Unfortunately, this only occurs in our dreams. Even though we don't recommend that you use these three shots as regulars in your game plan, we do feel it is important that you know how they are performed, so when the need arises, you know what to do.

THE DROP SHOT

A drop shot is a ground stroke that is hit so the ball barely clears the net and bounces twice before the opponent can get to it, or at least prevents the opponent from making an offensive shot. That's what makes the stroke so difficult. However, it's almost impossible to consistently hit drop shots that are difficult for the opponent to anticipate and return. Therefore, we recommend that you only attempt this shot when you are certain that you will still have the advantage in the point after the stroke has been hit. Now let's discuss how to hit a *winning* drop shot.

First of all, never hit a drop shot from behind the baseline. From that distance, the ball will stay in the air too long, and the opponent will have little difficulty reading what type of shot you've hit. Remember how important the ele-

The drop shot, usually considered a low percentage stroke, can be very effective if it is hit correctly. If not hit correctly, the opponent can easily take advantage of your mistake.

ment of surprise is. Wait for a ball that is shorter into your court, perhaps somewhere near the service line. Act as though you are going to hit a deep ground stroke or at least a penetrating approach shot. At the last instant, slow the velocity of your racket head and contact the ball so it has a bit of underspin and barely clears the net. Remember that you are attempting to hit the ball so it will bounce twice before the opponent can get to it. Also, don't let the ball go too high over the net. If the trajectory of the ball off the racket is too high, the bounce will also be too high, allowing the opponent more time to retrieve the shot. You can see from the photographs on page 96 that the racket face is slightly open and the action is slightly high-to-low. This causes the underspin and gives the ball the trajectory it needs to just make it over the net.

A rule of thumb to follow is to make the ball bounce at least five to seven times prior to its reaching the service line during your practice drills.

THE DROP VOLLEY

The next shot we consider risky is the drop volley. The objective of a good drop volley is the same as the drop shot, except that the ball is hit

before it bounces while you are in a net position. Disguise, in this case, is especially important. (See top of page 97.) If your opponent can easily read your drop volley while you are only eight to ten feet from the net, you are risking severe personal injury if the opponent tries to rip a ground stroke right through you! Also, any momentum that you have gained by being in an advantageous position at the net and attempting a low percentage drop volley is lost. However, there may be a time when you have pulled the opponent completely out of court and the opportunity for your drop volley is available. Therefore, here's what you need to do to hit the shot.

Prepare your racket as though you are going to hit your normal volley, whether it's a punch or a drive volley. Just as you are ready to hit the ball, slow the racket head so that the ball is hit with very little speed. (See bottom of page 97.) The purpose here is to barely clear the net and cause the ball to bounce twice before the opponent can reach it. Again, you don't want a drop volley to go very high over the net because the high trajectory will cause a high bounce, allowing the opponent more time to not only read the shot but also to get into an advantageous position for the return.

As you practice your drop volley, try to hit it

1

Rick Vetter demonstrates the precise movements involved in hitting an effective drop shot. He has hit the ball with slight underspin so it will bounce just over the net.

2

3

4

5

6

7

1

2

3

4

Butch Walts has hit an angled drop volley. Notice how his racket gives slightly after impact and how the ball travels so it will barely clear the net.

An effective drop volley must look as though you are going to drive the ball deep into the opponent's court. Work on disguising your volley, as shown here, and learn how to softly place it short in the opponent's court.

Rick Vetter illustrates how to disguise a good drop volley. Notice how he seems to be preparing for a normal volley but then lets up slightly on his forward swing, hitting the ball with little velocity.

so that it clears the net by very little margin and bounces from five to seven times before reaching the service line. But if you can do that consistently, you should be on the professional circuit—not reading this book!

THE HALF-VOLLEY

In this chapter, we've already talked about two highly controlled shots that usually have a very low percentage of success during competition. The next shot—the half-volley—is one that really doesn't have to be called a risky or low percentage shot; however, you probably should not plan in advance to use it. A half-volley occurs when you are in a net position and the ball is hit to you so that you can't hit a volley or take a step backward to hit your normal ground stroke. The half-volley is sort of a short "pickup" stroke that hits the ball on the rise immediately after it bounces from the court. This pickup shot isn't really a low percentage stroke, because usually you are forced to use it as the player below has. Obviously, you should volley the ball whenever you can, but it's a simple fact that sometimes you can't.

The half-volley takes place with a short

1

2

3

4

Here you see how a half-volley must be hit. The racket should not be taken back very far and the ball should be "picked-up" and directed to the part of the court you wish to hit it to. Here, Sue Arildsen has hit a half-volley.

backswing and contact ahead of the body if at all possible. As you can learn from Sue Arildsen in the photographs below, the racket face should be near vertical and the follow-through should go in the direction you wish the ball's flight path to follow.

Your preparation for the half-volley is extremely important. The knees must be bent and the seat must be low, keeping your eyes as close to the ball contact level as possible. This is often very difficult to do because half-volleys are hit so low, relative to the rest of the body. However, the lower you can get your eyes—within reason—the better off you'll be.

Many people feel that the half-volley is purely a defensive stroke and should be used only to keep the ball in play. Although you are often caught in a position where an aggressive half-volley is near to impossible, it doesn't have to be a defensive maneuver all the time. If you use this short pickup shot wisely, you can guide the ball deep into the opponent's court and lower the chances for an offensive return. In addition, a drop shot off a half-volley maneuver is not that difficult to hit. As with the other types of drop shots, though, it's difficult to be highly consistent and your percentage of winners may be extremely low.

1

2

3

4

Often, a player gets caught so she or he can't volley or hit a ground stroke. Sue Arildsen shows how the half-volley can help a player in this situation. Her racket face is near vertical and the follow-through guides the ball properly into the opponent's court. Here you can see how a short half-volley is hit.

Index